A farm in Tuscany

This Belongs to

_____

Medieval hilltown of Assisi

MICHAEL STORRINGS'
A PERSONAL RECORD BOOK
Italy
TRAVEL DIARY

PER VIA AEREA
PAR AVION

WARNER ⓦ TREASURES™
PUBLISHED BY WARNER BOOKS
A TIME WARNER COMPANY

Warner Treasures is a trademark
of Warner Books, Inc.

Warner Books, Inc.
1271 Avenue of the Americas
New York, N.Y. 10020

⑪ A Time Warner Company

Printed in China

First Printing: March 1995
10 9 8 7 6 5 4 3 2 1
ISBN: 0-446-91002-3

TABLE OF CONTENTS

L200 L200 ⑧ L5000 ITALIA

BUDGET

In Italy,
the unit of
currency
is the
lira

5067 U

⑨ L 500

L 500

L 50   L 50   L 100

L100   L 100

BANCA D'ITALIA

Gettone=200 lire

GETTONE

TELEFONICO

L 50

5000

Things my Friends
want me to do and see
10

A marble statue

Sicilian liqueur

Diane wears
size 38
Italian
shoes

Things to Bring back for my Friends and Family

Avete càmere libere?

Scalinata di Spagna

HOTEL

La
chiave

HOTEL F
* * *
Via Cesare R
(presso Stazio
80139 NAPOLI (ITALI
Telex 720
cod. Fisc. DFR MR
Partita I.V.A. O
RICEVUTA FISCAL

Camera 211
SIG RRINGS

conto 1

APPARTAMENTO/ROOM 50.000
PICCOLA COLAZI

⑯

PLACE BUSINESS CARDS HERE

TUTTI I CONFORTS

HOTEL
PENSIONE CA
ANGELO D

CORS

(17)

PLACE   BUSINESS   CARDS HERE

PLACE POSTCARD HERE

POSTCARDS
1-12
11Λ-09
HOTELS

PLACE   POSTCARD   HERE

COLAZIÓNE PRANZO

CÉNA

Restaurants

Avete una tàvola per due?

MENÙ

servizio incluso

ANTIPASTI

verdure ripiene

PRIMI PIATTI

risotto di mare

SECONDI PIATTI

bistecca alla griglia

CONTORNI

insalata mista

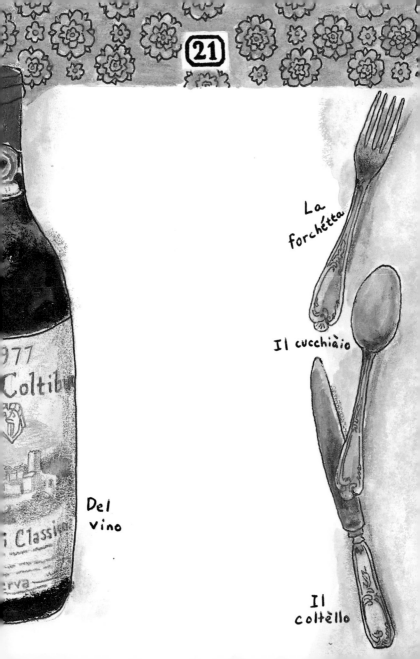

La forchétta

Il cucchiàio

Del vino

Il coltèllo

Farfalle

Fusilli

Spaghetti al Pomodoro

Antipasti

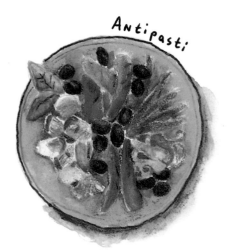

Penne rigate

Conchigliette

PIZZA MARGHERITA

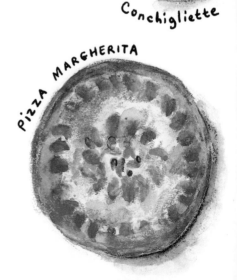

I BISCÒTTI

Camerière, il conto
per favore!

MERE
DEL DUCA
NAPOLI - Via A...
Cod. Fisc. DLD SVT ....
Dom. fisc. Strada Concordia, 14 N...
oli, lì

Natura, qualità e quantità
dei servizi

PANE E COPERTO

VINO

BIBITE

MINERALE

PLACE BUSINESS CARDS HERE

RISTORANTE

VIA GARI

PLACE BUSINESS CARDS HERE

New Friends

31

Caffè latte

Il camerière

Espresso

Il gatto

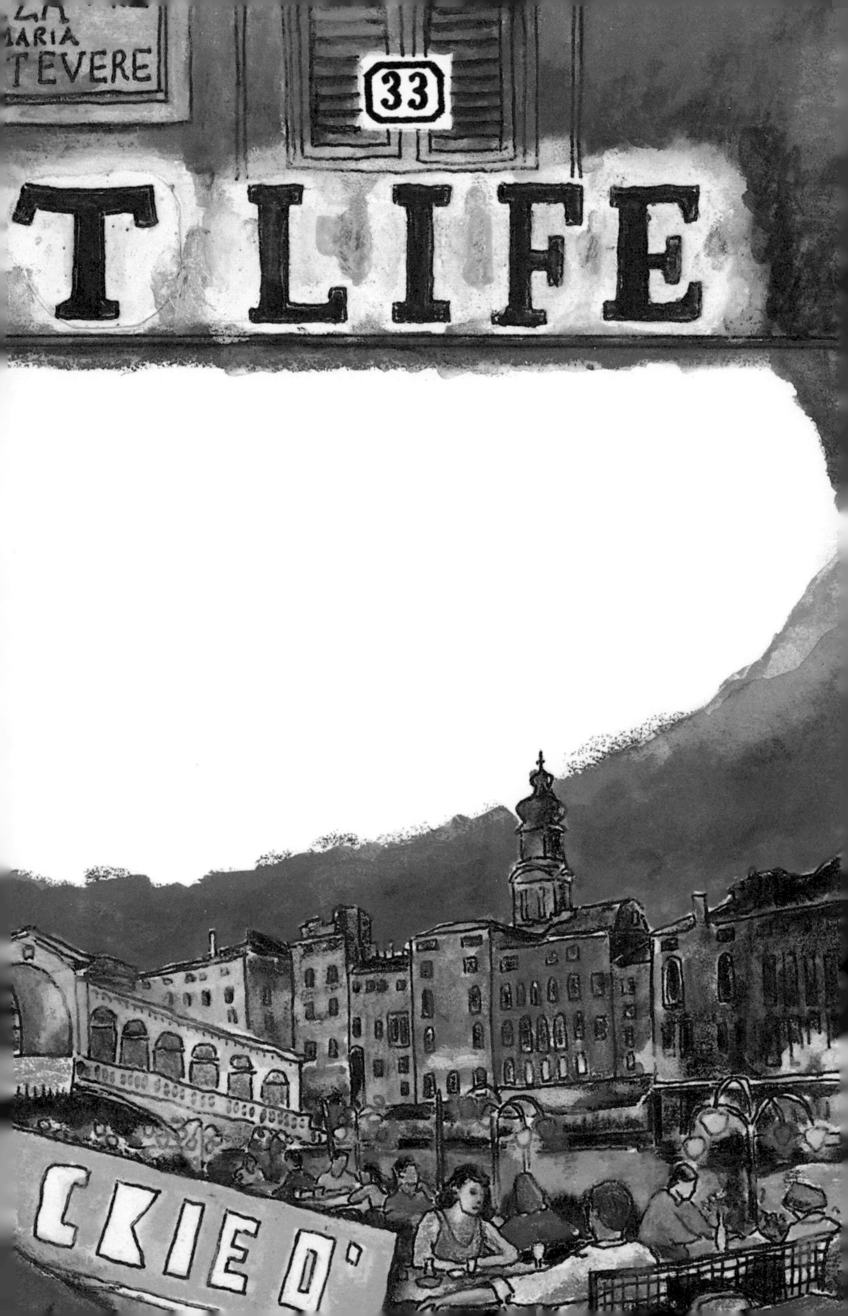

ZA
MARIA
TEVERE
33
T LIFE
CKIE D'

IL TEATRO

TEATRO A

LUNEDÌ 22 NO

CONCERTO STR

SERATA DEDICATA A
PER LA LOTTA CO

SOPRANO

MIRELLA FRE

AL TEATRO LA FENICE

SHOPPING NOTES

Quant'è per favore?

Blu

Vérde

Néro

Rósso

Giallo

Bianco

DRESS SIZES

U.S.	6	8	10
Italy	38	40	42

Vorrei...

Gioièlli

La Camìcia

Un'Anèllo

| 12 | 14 | 16 | 18 |
| 44 | 46 | 48 | 50 |

Giocàttolo

Questo=
This
one

Le Màschere della Venèzia

Murano
Glass

PLACE   BUSINESS   CARDS   HERE

41

PLACE BUSINESS CARDS HERE

The bell tower of San Lorenzo, Florence

No parking

Continua

Santa Croce, Florence

No
Stopping

SENSO UNICO

One-way
Street

No through road

strada
sensa uscita

Poggio on the island of ELBA

Siena

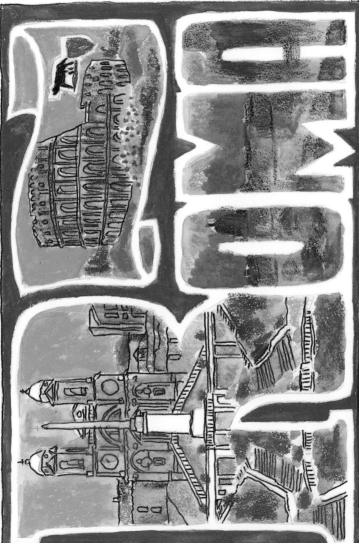

PLACE POSTCARD HERE

PLACE POSTCARD HERE

PLACE POSTCARD HERE

POSTCARDS
1-12
11A-09
1~~
ITALY

PLACE POSTCARD HERE

PLACE POSTCARD HERE

PLACE POSTCARD HERE